D0794527

DJUSD
Public Schools
Library Protection Act 2001

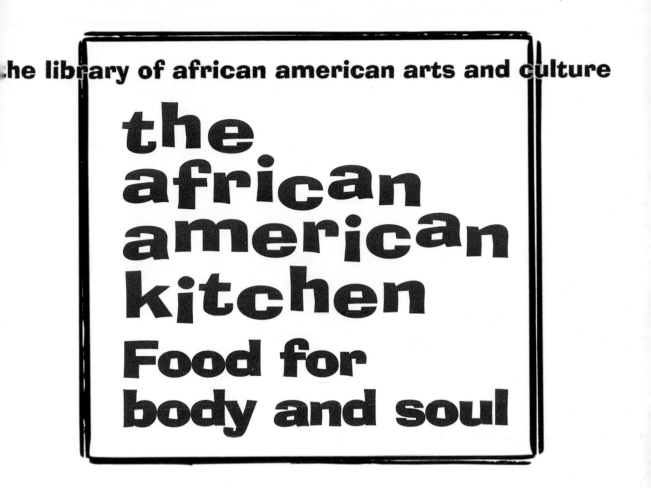

the african american kitchen

Food for body and soul

the library of african american arts and culture

the african american kitchen
Food for body and soul

george erdosh, ph.d.

rosen publishing group, inc./new york

Published in 1999 by The Rosen Publishing Group, Inc.
29 East 21st Street, New York, NY 10010

Copyright © 1999 by The Rosen Publishing Group, Inc.

First Edition

Library of Congress Cataloging-in-Publication Data

Erdosh, George.
    The African American Kitchen : food for body and soul / George Erdosh.
        p. cm. — (The library of African American arts and culture)
    Includes bibliographical references and index.
    Summary: Describes the influences on and the evolution of African
American cooking. Includes recipes and suggestions for healthy cooking.
    ISBN 0-8239-1850-5 (lib. bdg.)
    1. Afro-Ameriacn cookery—Juvenile literature. [1. Afro-American cook-
ery. 2. Cookery, American.] I. Title. II. Series.
TX715.E654 1999
641.59'296073--dc21   98-51814
                                                             CIP
                                                             AC

Manufactured in the United States of America

Contents

Introduction

Hungry? How about having some chicken and dumplings, gumbo, and fritters, and to top it all off, sweet corn pudding?

If you saw the movie *Soul Food* you probably know that African Americans have a rich tradition of cooking—rich in history, tastes, and hospitality. Food is what brings generations of people together.

This tradition spans hundreds of years, back to when Africans were brought to the New World as slaves. Though they lived here against their will and against all odds, the first African Americans thrived. Their traditions made a permanent change in American culture.

This book explores African American cooking. Over the years, it has brought New World cuisine to new heights. And new dishes are being created all the time!

Whether your tastes run to po'boys, sweet potato pie, or ribs, keep reading! Your hunger for food—and for knowing a people's rich history—will be more than satisfied.

In early history, foods were introduced to different cultures when people travelled. For example, Marco Polo was an early explorer who became famous for introducing Eastern spices to Europe.

A Short History of Cooking

Let's rewind for a moment. Thousands of years ago, before donut shops, grocery stores, fast-food joints, and supermarkets, our stone-age ancestors spent much of their time finding food. They hunted, fished, and gathered whatever they could find that was edible—plants, seeds, nuts, eggs, grubs, and insects—and came up with many ways to prepare it. They also had to find ways to preserve foods for days, weeks, or months, even in hot weather.

On the Move

At first, people cooked using the foods that grew around them. There was no transportation system to bring in foods from other areas. But, slowly, over time, merchants developed transportation systems with caravans of camels, mules, and horses. These caravans took new foods across continents and even from one continent to another. The change came even more rapidly in later centuries, when ocean transportation was established, and roads and railroads were built.

As people were introduced to new foods, their cooking began to change. For example, Europeans had no tomatoes, bell peppers, potatoes, and corn until Columbus brought them back from America where he found them as native plants. Later, the Portuguese introduced these vegetables to Africa. They also brought in another American vegetable, peanuts.

Each continent had its own native animals. These animals were introduced to the new lands

8 Africans were brought to America on slave ships, like the one at the right. Despite the cruel conditions of slavery, African Americans kept their traditions alive.

as well. For instance, chickens were originally native only to India. But once people from the rest of the world found out that chickens were easy to raise, they began to raise them.

American Cuisine

So how did we develop our American cuisine? It began with the Native Americans. Native Americans developed their own cuisine based on available foods, just like any other native group. The earliest immigrants to America came from England, Germany, and Holland in the 1600s. As these and other immigrants arrived from other parts of the world, they blended their own cuisine with what they found in America.

The African cuisine arrived in America with the African slaves. They worked the fields of the American South where English settlers farmed the land. Soon the foods of three groups—Native American, English, and African—blended into one. Over several generations, cooks kept adding new ingredients and seasonings and kept improving traditional cooking methods. In time, this became the famous traditional cuisine of the American South. In the chapters that follow, you'll read about how that change happened.

1 foods of africa

Before we check out African American cuisine, we will take a look at where it began—with the native foods of Africa.

The African continent is very large—about the size of North America—with many cuisines. The regions of Africa that influenced our own food heritage are: Tanzania, Kenya, and Ethiopia in the east part of Africa; Central African Republic and Chad in the center; Nigeria, Benin, Guinea, Ghana, and Congo in western Africa.

Native Food Is the Best Food

Each of Africa's hundreds of native cultures has its own unique foods. And over time, each culture developed its own distinct cooking styles.

Many traditions arose out of people's beliefs concerning the world around them. For example, some people refused to eat fish even though they lived near a large river. Fish were as disgusting to them as snakes or lizards are to us. In some cultures, chicken and eggs were sacred (like dogs and cats are in our society), and no one would eat them. Out of hundreds of edible plants around them, people selected only a few they considered acceptable.

The climate of Africa also influenced the type of foods that were grown and eaten. Compared to our North American climate, the climate of many regions of Africa is very unpredictable. Sometimes rains don't come for three or four years. Plants wither and animals starve. Then, suddenly, there are downpours and floods for months.

Over the centuries, African people adapted to their unpredictable climate. They learned that in order to survive in the dry years, they needed to dry and store excess food they grew in wet years. They learned many ways to preserve foods and to keep them safe for long periods of time.

Africans cultivated food plants differently than we do today. They mixed plants in their field in a way that looks random to us, instead of growing them in neat rows as today's farmers do. But this mingling of plants was not at all random—it was wise organic gardening! Plants help each other by exchanging soil nutrients. The taller, sun-loving plants provided shade to the lower, shade-loving crops. The closely-planted crop not only saved precious soil moisture but also reduced

African food from the four major food groups were:

Grains: wheat, barley, rice, millet, and sorghum (these two are local grains like wheat), but also sesame seeds cooked as grain.

Legumes: dried beans, lentils, and black-eyed peas.

Vegetables: various green leaves, which were always cooked (never raw like in salads), root vegetables, such as yams, taro roots, manioc (these two are starchy vegetables), beets, and egg plants.

Meat: goat, chicken, and fish with some beef and wild game.

weed and pest problems. The slaves carried this agricultural system to America, where it became known as their provision gardening. Once pesticides, fertilizers, and irrigation systems became widely used, provision gardening faded out.

Other native plants that were part of the African diet include coffee, lemons, olives, many tropical fruits, and sugar cane. The Portuguese introduced corn, tomatoes, chilies, peanuts, cassava (another root vegetable), and cocoa, all of which came from America with the Spanish explorers. They also brought new, better varieties of rice.

Many of these foods slowly became staples in the African diet. Corn became popular particularly fast. It was easy to grow, did well in poor soil and harsh climates, grew fast, tasted good, and could be stored for years. This helped guard against starvation in the dry years.

Getting Spicy

African cooking is vibrant with spices and seasonings. It has to be—most of the staple grains and legumes are almost flavorless without seasonings. Also, before refrigerators were invented, the hot, tropical climate of Africa made it necessary to enhance foods. By discouraging the growth of bacteria, spices helped to prevent food from spoiling!

Serving It Up

Food was prepared in many ways. One popular method of food preparation was cooking one-pot dishes over an open fire. Hearty and very nutritious stews and soups contained meat, chicken, or fish, several different vegetables, and sometimes grains. The ingredients would all simmer in a pot for hours.

Deep-frying in plenty of oil was also common. People deep-fried chunks of meat, fish, and almost any kind of vegetables, whole or in pieces, breaded or plain, until they turned brown, crisp, crunchy, and delicious—the way today's deep-frying transforms sticks of tasteless, raw potatoes into succulent french fries. They used palm oil squeezed from the berries of the palm

15

trees for deep-frying. Later, when the Portuguese introduced peanuts to Africa, Africans started to fry food in peanut oil.

Africans also roasted their food on an open fire, much as we do on barbecue grills. They dug pits in the ground, lined them with stones, built huge fires in them, and let fires burn down until only embers were glowing over the hot stones. They roasted meat, fish, and chicken over the embers. Or, they buried large chunks of meat in the hot embers for hours. The meat turned tender, juicy, and luscious inside and was sealed and protected by a black, crunchy crust outside.

In years of good rain, when there was plenty of extra food, people not only stored dried grains and legumes but also smoked or dried meat and fish for the leaner years.

Africans learned how to marinate and tenderize the tougher cuts of meat. Before roasting or cooking, they rubbed the meat with citrus juice, herbs, spices, onion, and chili and let it marinate for hours. The acid of the citrus juices turned the meat tender, and the spices made the meat flavorful.

2 africans in america

Beginning in the 1600s, Africans were captured by slave traders and brought to the New World to work as slaves. Brutally taken from their native land, they were packed onto slave ships that crossed the Atlantic. Even if they survived the trip, African captives were separated from their families and were made slaves for life. The slave system in the United States lasted until the Emancipation Proclamation freed slaves in 1863 and the American Civil War ended in 1865.

During the time of slavery, Africans worked on large farms called plantations that needed many field laborers. Slaves worked on rice and sugar plantations and, later, on cotton and tobacco farms. Soon, millions of slaves did all the field work in the American South.

New Foods

Food plants and seeds also came to America from Africa during this time. Many of these new plants were cultivated by slaves in provision gardens. Some plants did well in the new soil and climate; others did poorly. The food plants that did well became part of the slaves' main daily meal.

New foods from Africa included okra, watermelon, black-eyed peas, yam, eggplant, sesame seeds, several kinds of leafy greens, and African spices. Many food plants were introduced that originally came from South America but had traveled to Africa with the Portuguese. These included chilies (and other peppers), tomatoes, peanuts, and corn. Corn had already traveled to North America and was a staple food of the Native Americans in some areas, but the Africans re-introduced it.

Two New Drinks

Africa gave America two more gifts: coffee beans and kola nuts.

The first coffee beans came from a small native tree in Ethiopia. Coffee, the beverage brewed from the beans after they are roasted and ground, has been popular for at least one thousand years. America had coffee almost from the beginning of the European immigration. The English settlers in America were tea drinkers—but African coffee beans soon found their way into every American kitchen. Coffee soon became the most popular beverage in America.

Kola nuts came from West Africa. They contain chemical stimulants that make you forget how tired you feel and also suppress your appetite. Native Africans chewed these nuts to help over-come fatigue of hard work and long hours in the heat and to ignore their hunger when there was not enough food to eat.

There are similar, stimulating substances in coca leaves, which are native to the Bolivian area of South America, but they are even more powerful. Cocaine, an addictive drug, is extracted from coca leaves. South American Indians chewed these leaves for the same reasons the West Africans chewed kola nuts—to forget how tired and hungry they were, to deaden the aches and pains of their tough lives, and to make breathing easier in the thin air of the high mountains where they lived.

In 1886 an American chemist extracted these strange but natural substances from African kola nuts and South American coca leaves. He sold his concoction, dissolved in water, as medicine. He called it Coca-Cola.

It worked *too* well. People loved the effect of the various drugs in the new medicine, and they even liked the taste. Coca-Cola was a big success—but people soon realized it had harmful side effects. In 1903, the company removed the drugs in the the beverage but kept the original flavor.

Taking Root

As African food ingredients were introduced to America, so were African styles of food preparation. Africans in America cooked spicy one-pot meals, deep-fried many of their foods, and often roasted food on open fires. They also cooked and smoked meat by burying it in the glowing embers of a stove-lined barbecue pit. After slowly cooking leafy vegetables in water, they dipped cornbread in the pot to soak up the remaining nutrient-rich liquid. They called this pot likker (the word comes from pot liquor).

What the slaves did not have were meats of goat and wild animals that had been the center of meals in Africa. In America, they had a new meat, pork, which the land owners lived on. Soon, pork became the focal point of the slaves' meals too.

Okra-Tomato Rice Pilau

Rice pilau (called pilaf in the Middle East) is a true African dish. It's a rice dish made with onion and meat and often includes vegetables. Here, bacon is the meat flavoring, but you can use salt pork or meatless seasoning instead of bacon.

Ingredients

2 ounces lean thin-sliced bacon (about 2 slices), chopped

1 small yellow onion, peeled, finely chopped

1/2 pound okra, fresh or frozen, sliced

1 cup long-grain rice (raw)

1/2 tsp ground pure chili (not chili powder)

1 1/2 cups water

1/3 tsp salt

1/2 pound (2 medium) tomatoes, fresh or canned, coarsely chopped

Procedure

Sauté chopped bacon over medium heat in a large, heavy pan until crisp. Remove bacon with a slotted spoon and reserve on a small plate. Add onion to the fat. Sauté still on medium heat, for about 5 minutes, or until onion turns transparent, stirring occasionally. Add okra to the pan and continue to sauté for another 5 minutes, now stirring continuously. Add rice and chili and stir continuously for 3 minutes. Now, add water, salt, and tomatoes. When the mixture comes to a simmer, turn the heat low, cover the pan, and simmer for 15 minutes. Turn the heat off and let the pot sit covered for 5 minutes. Gently stir in the crisp bacon bits and serve with fresh cornbread and butter. Serves 4.

Originally wild peanuts only grew in tropical western Brazil and Bolivia. Natives in that area learned to cultivate them at least 3500 years ago. They slowly spread north to Mexico. The Spanish, who explored this region in the 1500s, took peanuts back to Spain from where they spread to Africa and Asia. Everyone loved them. They were easy to grow and cheap. Native American Indians brought peanuts north from Mexico. The first European immigrants in America found Indians already growing them in today's New England states. People didn't eat peanuts as snack food and peanut butter but boiled them for their main meal. Africans also brought peanuts with them to America. So, like corn, peanuts were introduced twice to America.

Gardening

African American slaves remained true to their gardening heritage by creating provision gardens. In America, provision gardens were especially useful because, although the slaves only had tiny plots of land, they still were able to grow several kinds of crops for their own use.

3 a new cuisine

Many slaves were able to keep a small kitchen garden and raise their own animals. And as a result, African Americans continued to experiment with new foods and create new styles of cooking.

More New Ingredients

Slaves commonly raised chicken and one or two pigs on their small plots of land. Plantation owners also gave their slaves the parts of pig that they didn't like: guts, snouts, ears, cheeks, bones, and much of the insides. Slaves used them to create flavorful stews.

With the addition of American ingredients, traditional African meals were slowly transformed. As years went by, the slaves' meals changed so much that their families back in Africa wouldn't have

An African American woman from King Street, Charleston, South Carolina, late 1800s.

recognized them. They
still used many African
plant foods: collard,
kale, turnip, mustard
greens, okra, yams, sweet
potatoes, peanuts, and rice.
But instead of using
smoked fish, goat,
and the meat of
wild game, they used
pork to flavor their food.
Slaves also gathered wild
foods to add variety to their
diet—fruits, nuts and animals they
could catch, mainly squirrels, rac-
coons, possums, and birds.
While they were not allowed to
hunt with guns, they became expert
trappers and fishermen.

Fresh okra

Some Changes

The way the African slaves cooked in America closely
resembled their African style. They cooked many
thick one-pot dishes to which they added whatever
food was available.

Fried foods were still a favorite. They fried
meats, fish, shellfish, vegetables, and even breads.

They often coated the food with cornmeal before frying it. Foods coated with a heavy batter and deep-fried were called fritters. A cook could make anything into a fritter by dipping it into batter and slipping it into hot fat. Fruits and vegetables were favorite choices for fritters.

In Africa, palm oil was used to deep-fry foods. Palm trees didn't grow well in the American South, so people switched to frying food in lard, the fat from the pig. Lard was easily available and plentiful. The high fat content of lard also provided slaves with energy needed for long and hard labor.

Fried okra-corn fritters

Plantation Cooks

Soon after slaves arrived in America, plantation owners brought many of them into their busy kitchens to help with the chores. The English plantation owners in the South needed extra help because they had a lavish

social life during the years of slavery. They entertained often and arranged big parties. Guests stayed at their large plantation homes for days and weeks.

Plantation owners were surprised at the versatile talents of the African kitchen helpers. Gradually, the slaves were given more responsibility and began taking over some of the cooking.

The plantation owners were amazed at how well the slaves prepared food. Suddenly, the bland English diet came alive with new tastes: stews with small amounts of well-flavored liquids, deep-fried meat, fish, and vegetables, light, moist cornbreads and biscuits, rice pilafs, wonderful, rich pies and puddings. The white plantation owners were cautious at first, but they came to like the new foods and jazzy cooking.

Soon, the slaves took over all the cooking duties. Though these cooks were slaves, in the kitchen they had all the freedom to use their imagination and skill to create. They were artists but were taken for granted.

English cooking began to change, but it didn't suddenly become African in the plantation kitchens. Rather, English, African, and Native American traditions were blended smoothly until a new cuisine evolved. This was the beginning of our famous Southern cooking. Cooks in Louisiana added the flavors of the French and Spanish cuisines, laying the foundation of the special New Orleans-style cooking, which we'll explore in Chapter 5.

30

4 migrating across the country

This blend of English, African, and Native American cooking remained in the South for about 150 years, during the era of slavery. African food did not yet reach tables in the rest of the country. European Americans didn't know (and didn't want to know) the foods of the African slaves, for these people and their customs were considered inferior.

This began to change in 1865, when slaves were freed by the Emancipation Proclamation. Very slowly, African Americans became part of the larger society of America, migrating from the South to the rest of the country. They carried their foods, cooking styles, and cooking skills, along with their meager possessions, north and west to the neighboring states. During the first half of the 1900s, the influence of African food slowly spread to the rest of America.

During the exodus of African Americans from Louisiana and Mississippi to St. Louis in 1879, a procession of refugees moves from the steamboat landing to the colored churches.

Slaves' Cooking Turns Popular

Soon, the country recognized that African Americans had an unexpected gift with foods and cooking. They could quickly learn to incorporate food ingredients they had not had in their own kitchens. They had the wonderful imagination and skills needed to create elegant, appealing, flavorful meals.

Former slaves who had worked as plantation cooks were in particular demand. Steamships, railway companies, restaurants, hotels, and wealthy families lured these cooks to their kitchens. Many cooks couldn't read or write. But they could bring out the best in any recipe,

Why we love deep-fried foods

Many complex chemical reactions take place when you heat foods to high temperature. It's called the browning reaction, and it is the most important chemical reaction in the kitchen. Whether you roast meat, barbecue ribs or hamburgers, deep-fry chicken or french-fries, bake bread, pizza, cookies or cake, you create new flavors through the browning reaction. When you deep-fry foods to golden brown, the hot oil starts the complex reactions that produce the irresistible flavors of fried foods.

jazz up food with seasonings, and balance a combination of ingredients. Foods came alive with flavor in their cooking pots.

The early American cooking inherited from English, German, Dutch, and Scandinavian immigrants was not especially flavorful. Their cooking style was simple, and the seasoning was minimal. The pleasing lift African spices and cooking techniques gave to American cuisine was a welcome change.

Southern Cooking

The foods these cooks created were not exactly the foods they cooked in their own simple kitchens. These were foods they created with African cooking techniques, spices, and flavorings but using the rich and varied ingredients available in America. Americans recognized this style of cooking as Southern cooking. Over the centuries of slavery, African cooking and Southern cooking became nearly the same.

If you ever had a crisp, nut-brown, perfectly deep-fried breaded chicken, or chicken gumbo and vegetable fritters; or still remember the taste of rich barbecued ribs with special home-cooked barbecue sauce; or have eaten a golden-brown, glossy pecan pie or a velvet-smooth sweet potato pie, then you know a bit about Southern cooking and the flavors of Africa.

Green Tomato Pie

Ingredients

Pie pastry for 9-inch double-crust
    pie, chilled
1 cup sugar
2 tbsp flour
1 tbsp cider vinegar
1 tbsp fresh lemon juice
1 tsp freshly grated lemon zest
1/2 tsp freshly grated nutmeg
2 tbsp melted butter
2 pounds green tomatoes, sliced very thin

Procedure

Divide the pie pastry into two, one piece slightly larger than the other. Roll out the large piece into a round that fits in a 9-inch pie pan with a little extra to drape over the edge. Fit the pasty in the pie pan. Keep the second half of pastry chilled.

Combine and mix the sugar and flour in one bowl, and the cider vinegar, lemon juice, lemon zest, nutmeg and melted butter in a second bowl.

Place the tomatoes over the pie pastry in the pan in a single overlapping layer. Sprinkle with some sugar-flour mix, then some of the second mixture. Continue layering the same way until all the tomatoes, sugar-flour mixture, and flavorings are used up.

Preheat the oven to 425°F. Roll out the second half of pastry so it covers and slightly overlaps the bottom pastry. With floured fingers pinch the edges together. Use a little water to moisten the crust if they don't seal well. Cut several vent holes in the top crust for the steam to escape.

Bake in the preheated oven for 20 minutes, then reduce temperature to 350°F and continue baking for 50 to 60 minutes or until the crust is golden. Best if served at room temperature.

Serves 6 to 8.

Virginia Crab Cakes

This recipe comes from the traditions of people living from New England to the Gulf Coast, who have developed recipes for everything from shrimp to crab to catfish.

In the region around Chesapeake Bay, crab is featured in many different recipes. These appetizer-sized crab cakes, originating in the Virginia Tidewater region, are one version of the famous Chesapeake crab cakes. Fresh bread crumbs can be used to coat the crab cakes. These crab cakes can be eaten with hot sauce, or made larger and served as a main course.

This recipe makes 2 dozen small crab cakes (or 8 large crab cakes)

Ingredients

2 Cups of fresh backfin crabmeat

1 Cup fresh, soft bread crumbs

2 eggs

1/2 Cup heavy Cream

Dash of Hot Sauce (or to taste)

2 tsps Worcestershire sauce

2 tsps chopped parsley

2 tsps grated onion

Salt and freshly ground black pepper, to taste

Butter for frying

Procedure

Pick over the crabmeat to remove any pieces of cartilage that may remain. Place the crabmeat and the bread crumbs in a bowl. In a separate bowl beat the eggs until light and then pour in the heavy cream. Slowly add the egg and cream mixture to the crabmeat and bread crumbs. Add the remaining ingredients, except the butter, and mix them in well. Correct the seasoning.

Melt 1 tablespoon of the butter in a heavy skillet over medium heat and drop the mixture into the skillet a tablespoon at a time. Cook, turning once, for 4 minutes or until golden brown on each side. Continue with the butter and ingredients until finished. Serve warm.

African American Cookbook

The first American cookbook was printed in 1742. Many others followed in the next 150 years but there wasn't a single African American cookbook among them. In fact, African cooking was ignored in all American cookbooks. There were no written-down recipes anywhere. This was not surprising since African Americans were forbidden to read or write when they were slaves.

Finally, in 1911, a well-known African American cook named Rufus Estes published the first African cookbook at his own expense. It's called *Good Things to Eat*. Rufus Estes recorded recipes in his book passed down from generation to generation by African cooks watching and learning in the kitchen.

The first cookbook was followed by many others. Today, we have many cookbooks to choose from!

soul food, creole, and cajun cooking

During the first half of the 1900s, the foods and cooking of African Americans were considered basic survival foods. But so were the foods of most immigrants. For example, pizza, a plateful of spaghetti with meatballs and a good tomato sauce, stuffed peppers, and Chinese stir-fried dishes all used to be thought of as second-rate immigrant dishes.

In the late 1960s, Americans developed a new interest in ethnic foods. Ethnic restaurants opened everywhere and became fashionable. African American cooking became popular, along with Asian, European, and Latin American food and cooking.

Soon African American cooking was part of the mainstream. Someone came up with a name—soul food—which has stuck ever since.

Sylvia's Restaurant in Harlem is known throughout the world for its soul food dishes.

What Is Soul Food?

Soul food is simple Southern cooking that black cooks prepare from available foods. The flavor depends on the cook's ability, not on fancy ingredients.

The meats in soul food include chicken parts, several kinds of fish, and parts of the pig not usually used by other cooks: snouts, jowls, ham hocks, innards, feet, hooves, tails, bones, and gristly meat. Soul food vegetables are easily-grown greens, such as collard, kale, mustard greens, and turnip and beet tops. Okra, deep-fried or stewed, is also part of the soul food kitchen. Rice and corn go well with the meal. The corn may be in the form of corn muffins or corn bread. Soul food also includes simple baking powder biscuits with gravy to dip the biscuits into. The gravy is made from lard, pan drippings, or bacon drippings. Hush puppies—deep-fried chunks of batter—are common on the soul food table, as are black-eyed peas or lima beans.

But the really necessary part of soul food is chittlin, originally called chitterlings. Chittlin is made from the small intestines of the pig. After thoroughly washing the intestines, a cook simmers the cut-up intestines with plenty of peppers, onions, spices, and other flavorings for about four hours until the meat turns soft. Chittlin is rich in fat, which gives the dish extra flavor.

Head cheese is another part of soul food. It is prepared by coarsely dicing the edible part of the pig's head, feet, and some other smaller meat pieces, and cooking these with spices until tender. When cooled, this dish turns the consistency of bologna.

Soul food also means the edible wild creatures that people trap, shoot, or catch for the meal: raccoon (simply called coon), squirrel, opossum (called possum), wild turkey, turtle, frog, fish, and shellfish. These wild creatures taste best when the meat is cooked into stews with vegetables and spices. But they are also good dipped into batter and deep-fried.

Soul food desserts are simply very sweet and very good: fruit cobblers and sweet potato or pumpkin pie with sorghum or corn syrup on top. Sometimes, a soul food meal ends with a simple sweet corn pudding.

Soul food is often made in large quantities, not just enough for a meal. There are large pots of stews and soups, buckets of crispy, deep-fried foods, bowls of gravy, several pies and puddings. Soul food in the South means hospitality—it is meant to be shared. Friends and

Chicken n' Dumplings

Ingredients

1 whole chicken (approx. 4 pounds)
1 large yellow onion, coarsely chopped
2 ribs celery, coarsely chopped
1/2 tsp salt (optional)
1/2 tsp freshly ground white pepper
1 bay leaf
1 cup chopped carrots
parsley (optional)

DUMPLINGS:

2 cups all-purpose flour
1/2 tsp salt (optional)
1/4 cup vegetable shortening, chilled

Procedure

Place chicken in large pot. Add about 2 quarts water, onions, celery, salt, pepper and bay leaf. Over high heat, bring to boil. Skim off foam. Reduce heat; cover, and simmer chicken until very tender, about 2

hours. Let chicken cool in broth.
Remove chicken from pot. Skim fat
from surface of broth. Strain broth
and return to pot; simmer to reduce
to about 1 quart.

Meanwhile, to make the dumplings:
In large bowl, combine flour and (if
desired) salt. Add vegetable shortening;
mix in with pastry blender or fork until mixture resembles coarse meal. Add just
enough chilled water (about 6 tablespoons)
to dough to make it the consistency of
piecrust dough. Bring chicken broth back to
boil; drop in spoonfuuls of dough, a few at a
time. When all dough strips are in pot, add
chicken. Reduce heat to low; simmer, uncovered,
until dumplings are done, about 35 minutes. During
cooking, occasionally stir gently,
just enough to keep dumplings
submerged and to prevent
those on the bottom from
sticking to pot. Makes 6
servings.

Why No Milk in Soul Food?

About 75% of Africans and African Americans are lactose intolerant (have trouble digesting milk). Only about 4% of Europeans have this problem. There is a reason for that!

Europeans enjoy a cooler climate than Africans so, in the days before refrigeration, they were able to keep milk longer. From early history they got into the habit of milking their dairy animals and eating dairy foods. However, Africa has a hot climate where milk and other perishable products spoil quickly. People couldn't keep dairy foods for long, so they didn't milk their cows and goats. Once children were weaned from mother's milk, they didn't drink milk anymore.

As a result, Africans stopped producing the enzyme, or chemical substance, that breaks down milk in their digestion. This change in body chemistry has been passed down for generations. And this is why you don't find many dairy products in soul food.

relatives may drop in and aren't allowed to leave until they are so full they can't eat another bite.

Cajun and Creole Foods

While soul food is purely African with strong American flavors, in Cajun and Creole cuisine, the flavors are more French with a strong African influence. Both cooking styles originated in Louisiana and spread to the rest of the country in the 1980s.

French food came to Louisiana in the 1700s, when the French moved from the Canadian province of Nova Scotia to Louisiana. Nova Scotia was called Acadia at that time, and these French settlers were called the Acadians. In French-Canadian pronunciation, *Acadian* sounds like *Cajun* to English-speaking people. So their cooking was called Cajun as well.

Cajun cooking is a mixture of French, African, and a little Native American. It is spicy but not very hot-spicy. It is the down-home cooking of the French-Canadian Americans—plain but tasty. In this regard, it is a lot like soul food.

Creole is a slightly more refined cooking style than Cajun. It developed in cities and is often served at fancy restaurants. Cooks at home cook Creole when they expect company. Like Cajun food, Creole food combines French, African, and some Native American influences. But it has, in addition, Spanish flavor (the Spanish were the first to colonize Louisiana). Creole is jazzy, well-spiced, and rather hot. It is full of flavor, full of zest, and full of music. Like African cooking, Creole cooking favors stews and soups and uses rice in many dishes.

The two most popular Creole dishes are jambalaya and gumbo. Both names came at least partly from Africa. Jambalaya is a combination of French and one African languages: *jambe* means shank in French; *a la*, also French, means of; and *ya* is rice in Africa. Gumbo came from a word in the African Bantu language, *kingombo*, which means okra.

Both jambalaya and gumbo begin with three all-important ingredients: onion, bell pepper, and celery.

Bread Pudding

In bread pudding, stale bread is toasted and cut into cubes, and is then transformed into a luscious dessert. As with rice pudding, you may choose to include raisins your bread pudding (or, of course, you can leave them out).

Ingredients

3 eggs
3 cups milk
1/2 cup sugar
1/2 pound stale white bread
1 cup dark raisins (optional)
1 tsp vanilla extract

Procedure

Preheat the oven to 350 degrees and butter a 1 1/2-quart baking dish or ovenproof casserole. In a medium-sized mixing bowl, beat the eggs until light. Add 2 1/2 cups of milk, all the sugar, and the vanilla to the eggs. Crumble the bread in a bowl and wet it thoroughly with the remaining 1/2 cup milk. Add the raisins (if using them) and put the bread mixture in the casserole. Pour the egg mixture over it, making sure that the ingredients are well mixed. Bake for 1 hour, or until lightly browned on top.

Serves 6.

Chicken Gumbo

The name gumbo comes from the African country Angola. In their language it was kingombo, which means okra. Now gumbo is a great Louisiana dish that you may serve as a thick stew or, with more liquid, as a soup.

Ingredients

1/2 cup vegetable oil, bacon drippings or combination

2 pounds boneless chicken meat, breast, thigh or combination

4 cups (1 pound) okra, fresh or frozen, in 1/2-inch slices

1 large onion (6 ounces), chopped

1/3 cup fresh parsley, chopped

1/3 cup celery tops, chopped

4 cups (2 pounds) tomatoes, chopped (canned or fresh if in season)

1 cup corn

1 cup rice

1 tsp salt

1/2 tsp fresh ground black pepper

1/2 tsp ground cayenne pepper

Procedure

Dry the chicken pieces well with paper towels. Heat the oil or bacon drippings in a heavy 3- or 4-quart pot over medium to high heat. Carefully slip the chicken pieces into the oil and saute' them, turning often, until golden brown in color, about 10 minutes. Don't crowd the pot; instead brown in two or three batches.

Take the chicken pieces from the fat with a slotted spoon; turn the heat down to medium.

Add the okra slices to the hot oil and, stirring often, brown them for 5 minutes. Remove the okra from the fat with a slotted spoon and reserve them next to the chicken.

Add the onion, parsley, and celery tops to the fat and brown until the onion turns golden, about 6 to 8 minutes. Stir often.

Add the tomatoes, salt, pepper, cayenne and return the browned chicken to the pot with 3 cups of water. Stir well, bring the stew to a slow boil, then turn the heat down low and cover the pot. Simmer for 20 minutes. You may add 2 or 3 cups more water to make a chicken gumbo soup instead of a stew.

Stir the okra into the stew, cover and continue to simmer for 20 minutes. Stir occasionally.

Serve over fresh-cooked rice with warm, fresh-baked cornbread.
Serves 8.

Tomato is very common too. In jambalaya, the key ingredient is rice, while in gumbo, it's okra. Both dishes are spiced with dried red chili, black pepper, garlic, bay leaf, basil, thyme, and parsley. To these basic ingredients, cooks add either chicken, meat, fish, or shellfish. They also can be made meatless, with extra fresh vegetables. There is an African-style, meatless gumbo, similar to cooked greens with pot likker in soul food, that is called *gumbo z'herbes*. It's different from pot likker in that it is highly spiced with typical gumbo ingredients.

African American cooking has gone through many changes in its long history. And it continues to change all the time.

One change is occurring because peoples' nutritional needs are different than they were in earlier centuries. Centuries ago, hard physical labor was part of peoples' daily lives. When African Americans were slaves in America, their physical labor was harder, and work lasted from sunrise to sunset or even longer. To do these long hours of physical work, the human body needs plenty of fuel, just as a car you drive all day needs plenty of gas.

Foods give the human body its fuel. All foods are made up of four parts: proteins, starches, fats, and water. Proteins build muscles; fats and starches provide energy to fuel physical work.

To fuel their bodies, African Americans ate

Scrambled Tofu with Tortillas and Black Beans

Ingredients

1 tbsp butter
1 tbsp vegetable oil
1/2 cup chopped yellow onion
1/2 cup chopped green bell pepper
2 corn tortillas, halved, cut into 1/2 inch
      wide strips
1 lb. medium or firm tofu, sliced, drained well
1/2 tsp tumeric
1/4 tsp salt (optional)
1/8 tsp ground white pepper
2 cups cooked black bean
Sauce (below):
8-ounce can salt-free (or regular) tomato
1 tbsp chopped fresh cilantro
1/2 tsp ground cumin
1/8 tsp garlic powder

Procedure

Heat butter and oil in large non-stick skillet over medium heat. Add onion and bell pepper. Cook, stirring frequently, about 5 minutes.

Add tortillas; continue to cook until onions are lightly browned, about 3 additional minutes. Meanwhile, place tofu in a large bowl and mash with a fork. Add turmeric, salt (if desired), and pepper; mix well.

To make sauce, in small saucepan, combine all the sauce ingredients; heat until hot and bubbly. Add tofu mixture to browned onions and tortillas. Cook, stirring frequently, until heated through. To serve, spoon tofu mixture onto 4 serving plates; top with sauce. Serve with black beans. Makes 4 servings.

food high in fat and starches: deep-fried meats and vegetables, the fattiest parts of the pig, starchy vegetables, and breads. They replenished their protein needs from meat, seeds, grains, and nuts. Yet no one became overweight! The energy they took in as fats was used up in the long hours of work.

A Change In Lifestyle

Heavy physical work for African Americans continued through the middle 1900s. Life then became easier. Machinery replaced heavy physical work, and the long working hours were reduced. But the traditional food never changed much. It was still high in fats, and people were still used to eating plenty. When there is more energy going into the body than is used up, the extra energy is stored as fat, and people become overweight.

Traditional eating habits are not easy to change. What your grandparents and parents eat, you eat too. And traditional soul food is high in fats, cholesterol, salt, and sugar. So fatty, high-starch foods remained on the table and in the 1960s and 1970s, people had an increasing number of health problems.

Eating Healthier

In the 1990s, though, most Americans became knowledgeable about healthy diets. With little physical work, and much leisure time, we are changing our foods to have lower fat content, lower cholesterol, and less sugar. We are eating more vegetables and fruits.

Go to any bookstore, pick up any magazine, and you can see an abundance of African American recipes for today's taste. The influence of African food is still strong in America, and today, it's appreciated throughout the country. African American kitchens are also adopting the ingredients of other cultures and coming up with delicious results.

The African American kitchen is one of our oldest traditions. It is our heritage.

browning reaction Chemical reaction when food is deep-fried.

Cajun cooking Style of cooking, combining African, French, and Native American influences, that originated in Louisiana.

chittlin Originally called chitterlings; the signature dish of soul food.

Creole cooking Also known as New Orleans-style cooking; a refined cuisine that mixes African, Native American, Spanish, and French traditions.

food groups Types of food—grains, legumes, vegetables, and meats—essential to a healthy diet.

gumbo Creole dish made with okra.

jambalaya Creole dish made with rice.

lactose intolerance Difficulty digesting milk.

marinate Use of spices and citrus juices to preserve and flavor meat.

provision gardening System of land cultivation brought to America by African slaves.

soul food Simple, home-style Southern cooking.

Southern cooking Tradition of cooking, based on African traditions, that developed in the American South during the slave era.

For Further reading

Albyn, C.L. and L.S. Webb. *The Multicultural Cookbook for Students*. Phoenix, AZ: Oryx Press, 1993.

Cusick, H.H. *Soul and Spice: African Cooking in the Americas*. San Francisco: Chronicle Books, 1995.

Harris, J.B. *Iron Pots and Wooden Spoons: Africa's Gift to New World Cooking*. New York: Ballantine Books, 1989.

Krondl, M. *Around the American Table*. Holbrook, MA: Adams Publishers, 1995.

Lee, H.G. *Taste of the States: A Food History of America*. Charlottesville, VA: Howell Press, 1992.

McIntosh, E.N. *American Food Habits in Historical Perspective*. Westport, CT: Praeger, 1992.

Prudhomme, P. *Chef Paul Prudhomme's Louisiana Kitchen*. New York: William Morrow & Co., 1984.

Wilson C.R. and W. Ferris, eds. *Encyclopedia of Southern Culture*. Chapel Hill, NC: University of North Carolina Press, 1985.

Here is a good West African recipe book written for American kids:

Ossea-Asare, F. *A Good Soup Attracts Chairs: A First African Cookbook for American Kids*. Gretna, LA: Pelican Publishing Co., 1993.

Where to Get African American Food

Most of the ingredients for African American cooking are readily available in any well-stocked supermarket. For any uncommon ingredient, you probably can find it in a market within an African American community. You also can obtain ingredients through mail-order:

Ken Davis Barbecue Sauce
Ken Davis Products, Inc.
4210 Park Glen Road
Minneapolis, MN 55416
(612) 922-5556

Hoppin' John Taylor
30 Pinckney Street
Charleston, SC 29401
(803) 577-6404

The New Orleans School of Cooking and Louisiana General Store
620 Decatur St.
New Orleans, LA 70130
(800) 237-4841

Virginia Smalls
1091 Greenhill Road
Charleston, SC 29412

Index

a
African-American cookbook, 39
African native cooking, 11–14

b
barbecue, 16, 33
bread pudding, 48–49
browning reaction, 32

c
Cajun coking, 46–47
chicken gumbo, 50–52
chicken n' dumplings, 44–45
chittlin (chitterlings), 43
Coca–Cola, 21
coca leaves, 20–21
coffee, 19–20
corn, 8, 14, 19, 42
Creole cooking, 29, 46–47, 53

d
deep–frying, 15–16, 26–27, 32

f
food preservation, 12, 14, 17
fritters, 26–27

g
green tomato pie, 34–35
gumbo, 47, 53

h
health and diet, 58–59
hush puppies, 42

j
jambalaya, 47

k
kola nuts, 19–20

l
lactose intolerance, 46

o
okra–tomato rice pilau, 22–23

p
peanuts, 8, 16, 24
plantation cooks, 27–29
pot likker, 21, 53
provision gardening, 12–13, 19, 24

s
scrambled tofu with tortillas and black beans, 56–57
slave cooking, 18–19, 31, 33
soul food, 41–46, 59
spices, 14, 26
stone–age cooking, 7–8
super–rich Virginia crab cakes, 36–38

t
transportation and new foods, 8

w
wild game, 21, 26, 43

Acknowledgments

The author gratefully acknowledges the use of the library facilities in which he did his research: the University of California, Davis, and California State University, Sacramento.

About the Author

George Erdosh received his formal education at McGill University in Montreal. After running a catering business in Sacramento, California, he began culinary science writing. The author of the *Cooking Throughout American History* series for PowerKids Press, George Erdosh lives in Pine Grove, California, with his wife.

Photo Credits

Cover photo by Les Mills, (background) © StockFood America. Pp. 2, 54 © Everett Collection; pp. 4, 27, 33, 37, 38, 42, 44, 48, 50 © StockFood America; pp. 7, 30 © Corbis Bettman; pp. 8, 20, 25 © Archive Photos; pp. 10, 16, © FPG International; pp. 13, 24, 26, 32, 35, 45, 49 © International Stock Photo; pp. 13, 15, 22, 23, 24, 34, 35, 46, 50 , 51, 52, 56, 57 © 1995 PhotoDisc, Inc.; pp. 18-19 © Photographs and Prints Division, Schomburg Center for Research in Black Culture, The New York Public Library, Astor Lenox and Tilden Foundations; p. 28 courtesy of Hampton University Archives; p. 39 by Christine Innamorato; p. 40-41 by Debra DiPeso.

Design and Layout

Laura Murawski

Consulting Editors

Erin M. Hovanec and Erica Smith